TIME

MANAGEMENT

GUIDE

FOR

COLLEGE STUDENTS

27 Proven Steps to Increase Productivity, Overcome Procrastination, Accomplish More in Less Time, Have Fun and Balance College Life

Twilight Publications

and exhausted. Here, we will dive into effective prioritizing techniques, time-blocking, and the art of saying no. As you dig deeper into the next chapters, you'll discover how technology can improve your time management skills.

Conscious use of technology can be a powerful ally in your quest for efficiency and productivity. We'll explore digital calendars, productivity apps, and tools designed to eliminate distractions and improve focus.

In addition, we will explore self-reflection and self-care. Time management is more than just checking off tasks on a to-do list. It's about understanding your strengths, limitations, and values. We'll guide you through the process of discovering your unique rhythm and design a time management system that fits your individual needs and aspirations.

Now, dear reader, it's time to embark on this transformative journey together.

"Time Management Guide for College Students" is more than just a collection of theories and concepts. It is an invitation to take control of your destiny. It is a roadmap to unlocking your full potential and striking a harmonious balance between academic pursuits, personal growth, and a vibrant social life. As you turn each page, allow yourself to dream big. Envision a future where time becomes your ally, not your enemy. Prepare to be inspired, motivated, and captivated by the stories of college students who have transformed their lives through effective time management. Embrace the challenges ahead, knowing that the journey itself holds the key to unlocking your true potential.

Are you ready to seize control of your destiny? Time is running out and the choice is yours.

Join me on this exhilarating quest, and together we will unravel the secrets to conquering time and unleashing your greatness in college life. Let the journey begin!

Goal Setting and Priorities for College Students

"Lost time is never found again."

- Benjamin Franklin –

I n the vast landscape of college life, filled with endless possibilities and demanding responsibilities, one crucial element stands tall as the guiding force—goal setting. As a college student, understanding the power of goals and learning how to set them effectively is a fundamental skill that will shape your path to success. In this chapter, we will delve into the transformative realm of goal setting and priorities, unveiling the secrets to achieving academic excellence and personal growth through strategic time management.

Understanding the Power of Goals

Goals are like stars guiding us through the darkness, illuminating the path towards our desired future. They provide clarity, focus, and a sense of purpose in our daily lives. In the realm of college, where time is a precious commodity, goals become even more crucial. They act as beacons, steering us towards academic achievements, personal development, and a well-balanced lifestyle.

Without clearly defined goals, we risk drifting aimlessly, swayed by distractions and overwhelmed by the multitude of tasks that come our way. Setting goals empowers us to take control of our destiny, creating a roadmap for success. It allows us to channel our energy and efforts towards what truly matters, making the most of our limited time and resources.

An Example of Bad Goal Setting

To understand the impact of effective goal setting, let's examine an example of bad goal setting:

*Joseph, a college student, sets a vague goal of **"getting good grades."** While the intention is admirable, the lack of specificity and clarity hinders his progress. Joseph finds himself lost, unsure of what actions to take to achieve his desired outcome. As a result, he becomes overwhelmed and frustrated, unable to make meaningful progress towards his goal.*

Setting SMART Goals for Academic Success

To avoid the pitfalls of ambiguous goals, we introduce the concept of SMART goals.

SMART stands for *Specific, Measurable, Achievable, Relevant, and Time-bound*. When applied to goal setting, these principles provide a solid framework for success.

Let's revisit Joseph's goal of **"getting good grades"** and transform it into a SMART goal.

Joseph reframes his goal to "Achieve a GPA of 3.5 or higher in the current semester by attending all classes, completing assignments on time, and seeking assistance from professors when needed."

This SMART goal is specific, as it clearly outlines the desired outcome and the actions required to achieve it.

It is measurable, as Joseph can track his progress by monitoring his grades.

It is achievable, as it takes into account his capabilities and available resources.

It is relevant to his academic success, and it is time-bound, focusing on the current semester.

By setting SMART goals, you create a roadmap that guides your actions and measures your progress. It provides a sense of direction and purpose, making your journey through college more focused and intentional.

Whether it's improving your GPA, mastering a challenging subject, or securing an internship, SMART goals become your compass, ensuring that you make the most of your time and efforts.

Prioritizing Tasks and Activities Based on Importance

With goals in place, the next step is to prioritize tasks and activities based on their importance and alignment with your objectives. College life presents a myriad of responsibilities, from attending classes and completing assignments to engaging in extracurricular activities and maintaining a social life. It is easy to feel overwhelmed and pulled in multiple directions.

To effectively manage your time, it is crucial to prioritize tasks based on their significance. Not all tasks hold equal weight in contributing to your overall goals and aspirations.

By identifying the high-priority tasks and allocating time and energy accordingly, you ensure that your efforts are aligned with what truly matters.

To illustrate the importance of prioritization, *let's consider the example of Mark, a college student who wants to excel academically while also participating in various clubs and organizations. Without prioritization, Mark finds himself overwhelmed and unable to balance his commitments. His grades suffer as he spreads himself too thin, trying to do everything at once.*

By implementing effective prioritization strategies, Mark can regain control of his time and energy.

He identifies his academic success as a top priority and allocates dedicated study hours, ensuring that he devotes sufficient time to his coursework. He then evaluates his extracurricular activities and makes strategic choices based on their alignment with his long-term goals.

In prioritizing tasks, it is essential to distinguish between urgent and important activities. Urgent tasks demand immediate attention, but they may not necessarily contribute significantly to your long-term goals.

On the other hand, important tasks align with your objectives and have a lasting impact on your academic and personal growth. By focusing on the important tasks, you ensure that your time and efforts are optimized for success.

By setting SMART goals and prioritizing tasks effectively, you lay the foundation for effective time management in college. You unlock the power to steer your journey towards academic excellence, personal growth, and a fulfilling college experience.

Specific Steps to Setting SMART Goals for Academic Success

Step 1: Reflect on Your Long-Term and Short-Term Goals.

Take the time to reflect on your aspirations and what you want to achieve in both the long-term and short-term. Consider your academic goals, career aspirations, personal development, and any other areas of importance to you.

Ask yourself questions like:

1. *What do I want to accomplish by the end of this semester or academic year?*
2. *What are my long-term career goals and how can my academic success contribute to them?*
3. *What skills or knowledge do I want to gain during my college journey?*
4. *How can I achieve a healthy work-life balance while pursuing my goals?*

Reflecting on these questions will help you gain clarity and define your goals more specifically.

Step 2: Write Down Your Goals and Display Them in a Visible Place.

Once you have identified your goals, write them down in a clear and concise manner. Be precise about your objectives and set measurable goals.

For example, if your goal is to improve your GPA, specify the target GPA you want to reach. If your goal is to secure an internship, define the specific companies or industries you want to target.

After writing down your goals, display them in a visible place where you can see them regularly. This could be on a whiteboard in your study area, on sticky notes on your desk, or as the wallpaper on your computer or phone. Keeping your goals visible serves as a constant reminder of what you're working towards and helps maintain your focus and motivation.

Step 3: Rank Your Tasks Based on Their Importance and Create a Priority List.

To effectively prioritize tasks and activities, start by evaluating their importance in relation to your goals. Consider which tasks will have the most significant impact on your academic success and personal growth.

Ask yourself:

1. *How does this task contribute to my short-term or long-term goals?*
2. *Will completing this task help me make progress towards my desired outcomes?*
3. *What are the consequences of not prioritizing this task?*

Once you have evaluated the importance of each task, create a priority list. Rank your tasks in order of importance, placing the most critical tasks at the top. This will guide your focus and ensure that you allocate your time and energy to the tasks that align with your goals and have the greatest impact.

As you work through your priority list, be mindful of deadlines and timelines associated with each task.

Break down larger tasks into smaller, manageable subtasks, allowing you to make steady progress.

Regularly review and adjust your priority list as new tasks or responsibilities arise, ensuring that you stay aligned with your goals and adapt to changing circumstances.

By following these actionable steps, you will be well on your way to setting SMART goals for academic success and effectively prioritizing tasks and activities.

Remember, the key lies in reflection, clarity, and maintaining a visible reminder of your goals. With a clear focus on what truly matters, you can make the most of your time in college and achieve your desired outcomes.

Finally, as a college student, your time is a precious resource. By harnessing the power of goals and priorities, you will unleash your potential and create a meaningful and successful college journey. Stay committed, stay focused, and let your goals be the guiding stars that illuminate your path.

Creating a Personalized Schedule

"Time is the coin of your life. It is the only coin you have, and only you can determine how it will be spent Be careful lest you let other people spend it for you."

- Carl Sandburg -

T ick-tock, tick-tock. Time marches on, unforgiving and relentless. As college students, we find ourselves at the crossroads of endless opportunities and demanding responsibilities. The key to navigating this tumultuous journey lies in the mastery of time management. In this chapter, we will embark on a transformative quest to create a personalized schedule—a powerful tool that will unlock your potential and empower you to make the most of your college experience.

The Benefits of Having a Schedule

Imagine a world where chaos gives way to order, where uncertainty is replaced by structure. This is the world of a well-crafted schedule. Having a schedule is more than just a practical tool; it is a gateway to efficiency, productivity, and a sense of control over your time.

By creating a personalized schedule, you gain several key benefits:

Organization: A schedule provides a clear framework for your day, helping you stay organized and on track. It ensures that you allocate time for essential tasks and activities, reducing the likelihood of procrastination and last-minute rush.

Time Optimization: With a schedule in place, you can optimize your time by allocating it to activities that align with your goals and priorities. By eliminating time wasted on indecision or unproductive pursuits, you free up valuable hours for meaningful engagement.

Reduced Stress: When you have a clear plan and know what to expect, it alleviates the stress and anxiety that can accompany a disorganized or overwhelming schedule. A schedule provides a sense of structure and certainty, allowing you to approach each day with confidence.

How to Create a Daily, Weekly, and Monthly Schedule

Creating a personalized schedule involves careful consideration of your commitments, goals, and the unique rhythm of your life. It is a dynamic process that requires regular review and adjustment. Let's explore how you can create schedules at different time intervals:

Daily Schedule:

Start by outlining your fixed commitments, such as classes, work, or extracurricular activities. Assign specific time slots for each of these activities, considering their duration and any necessary travel time.

Next, identify your priorities for the day. What tasks or activities are most important to accomplish? Block out dedicated time for these tasks, ensuring that they align with your goals and contribute to your overall success.

Remember to include breaks and downtime in your daily schedule. Taking regular breaks improves focus and prevents burnout. Allocate time for meals, exercise, relaxation, and self-care to maintain a healthy work-life balance.

Weekly Schedule:

A weekly schedule allows you to plan for recurring commitments and long-term goals. Start by reviewing your class schedule and identifying any consistent time blocks for studying or completing assignments.

Allocate specific time slots for each course, considering the workload and the importance of each subject. Ensure that you distribute study time evenly across the week to maintain a balanced approach.

Additionally, include time for extracurricular activities, such as club meetings, sports practices, or volunteering. These activities enrich your college experience and contribute to personal growth.

Monthly Schedule:

A monthly schedule provides a broader perspective, helping you plan ahead for major assignments, exams, and other important events. Mark important deadlines, projects, and exams on your calendar to ensure that you have ample time to prepare and avoid last-minute stress.

Consider your long-term goals and aspirations. Are there any specific tasks or projects you need to work on over an extended period? Break them down into smaller, manageable tasks and allocate time for them throughout the month.

Including Study Time, Classes, Extracurricular Activities, and Personal Time in Your Schedule

A well-rounded college experience encompasses not only academic pursuits but also extracurricular activities, social engagements, and personal time. To create a balanced schedule, it is crucial to allocate time for each of these areas. Here's how:

Study Time:

Studying is a fundamental part of your college journey. Dedicate focused blocks of time in your schedule for studying each day. Find a study environment that suits your preferences and promotes concentration. Eliminate distractions during study sessions to maximize productivity.

Consider your energy levels and personal preferences when planning study time. Some students thrive in the mornings, while others are more productive in the afternoons or evenings. Tailor your schedule to your individual needs for optimal results.

Classes:

Your class schedule forms the backbone of your daily routine. Allocate specific time slots for each class, including time for transportation if necessary. Arriving early for classes allows you to settle in and be fully present for the learning experience.

Extracurricular Activities:

Extracurricular activities are an essential part of college life, offering opportunities for personal growth, skill development, and social connections. Whether it's joining clubs, participating in sports, or engaging in community service, allocate dedicated time for these activities in your schedule. Consider their time requirements and ensure they align with your priorities.

Personal Time:

Taking care of your well-being is crucial for success in college. Allocate time for self-care activities, such as exercise, hobbies, relaxation, and socializing with friends. Prioritize personal time to recharge, reflect, and maintain a healthy work-life balance.

Remember, your schedule is a flexible tool that can be adjusted as needed. Be open to adapting it based on changing circumstances and unforeseen events. Regularly review your schedule to ensure it remains aligned with your goals and priorities.

As you create your personalized schedule, remember that it is a reflection of your commitment to personal growth, academic success, and overall well-being. Embrace the structure it provides and let it guide you towards a balanced and fulfilling college experience.

Actionable Steps Needed to Create a Personalized Schedule

Creating a personalized schedule is a powerful tool that can revolutionize your time management skills. It allows you to prioritize your commitments, allocate time for essential tasks, and strike a balance between academic pursuits, extracurricular activities, and personal time.

To achieve an effective and personalized schedule, follow these steps:

Determine Your Ideal Study Hours and Allocate Them in Your Schedule:

i.   Take a moment to reflect on your optimal study hours.

ii.   Consider your energy levels, concentration abilities, and personal preferences.

Are you a morning person or do you work better at night?

iii.   Determine what time of day you are the most focused and alert.

iv.   Once you've determined your ideal study hours, allocate dedicated blocks of time in your schedule for studying.

v.   Whether it's early mornings, afternoons, or evenings, designate specific time slots where you can fully dedicate yourself to academic work.

vi.   Treat these study periods as non-negotiable appointments with yourself.

Map Out Your Classes, Activities, and Other Commitments on a Weekly/Monthly Calendar:

To create a comprehensive schedule, start by mapping out your classes, extracurricular activities, work, and other commitments.

Begin with a weekly calendar and mark the days and times of your classes.

Add any recurring commitments such as club meetings, sports practices, or part-time job shifts.

Next, consider important deadlines, exams, and projects. Mark these dates on your calendar to ensure that you have sufficient time to prepare and complete them. By visualizing your commitments, you gain a clear overview of your time availability and potential scheduling conflicts.

For a more long-term perspective, extend your schedule to a monthly calendar.

This allows you to plan ahead for major assignments, exams, and other important events. As you populate your calendar, ensure that you allocate sufficient time for each commitment and maintain a balanced distribution of activities throughout the week.

Adjust and Refine Your Schedule as Needed to Find the Right Balance:

Creating a personalized schedule is an ongoing process that requires flexibility and adjustment. Monitor your schedule regularly and assess how well it aligns with your goals, priorities, and overall well-being. Be open to making changes and refinements as needed.

Evaluate your time allocation and assess whether certain activities or tasks are taking up more time than necessary. Look for opportunities to streamline your schedule and eliminate any time-wasting activities or distractions. Keep in mind that finding the right balance may require making difficult decisions and prioritizing your most important commitments.

Be mindful of your energy levels and overall well-being. If you find that your schedule is leaving you overwhelmed or burnt out, make adjustments to create more space for self-care and relaxation.

Remember, a well-crafted schedule should support your academic success while also nurturing your personal growth and well-being.

As you implement these actionable steps, remember that creating a personalized schedule is a dynamic process. Be willing to experiment, adapt, and refine your schedule as you discover what works best for you. With perseverance and a commitment to time management, you will unlock the power of a personalized schedule and maximize your potential in college and beyond.

Breaking Tasks into Manageable Chunks

"Success is the sum of small efforts, repeated

day in and day out."

- Robert Collier –

T asks and responsibilities can often feel overwhelming. From complex assignments to long-term projects, it's easy to become paralyzed by the sheer magnitude of the work ahead.

However, there is a powerful technique that can alleviate this sense of overwhelm and empower you to conquer any task: breaking them down into manageable chunks. In this chapter we will explore the art of task breakdown and discover techniques to organize and schedule smaller tasks effectively.

Understanding the Concept of Task Breakdown

Task breakdown is the process of dividing a larger task or project into smaller, more manageable parts. By breaking down complex tasks, you can approach them with clarity, focus, and a sense of progress. This technique allows you to overcome procrastination, maintain motivation, and ultimately achieve your goals more efficiently.

When faced with a daunting task, it's common to feel overwhelmed and unsure of where to begin. Breaking it down into smaller chunks not only simplifies the work but also provides a clear roadmap to follow. Each smaller task becomes a growth and should be scheduled and planned for.

iii. **Urgent but Not Important** (Delegate): Tasks in this quadrant are urgent but do not contribute significantly to your long-term goals. They are usually time-sensitive and require attention, but they can be delegated to others if possible.

iv. **Not Urgent and Not Important** (Eliminate): The task in this quadrant is neither urgent nor important. They are time-wasters and distractions that should be eliminated or minimized to free up time for more meaningful activities.

The Eisenhower Matrix helps individuals identify which tasks deserve their immediate attention and which can be postponed or delegated. By using this matrix, individuals can enhance their productivity, focus on high-priority tasks, reduce stress, and achieve a better work-life balance.

To effectively use the Eisenhower Matrix, you can list all your tasks and then categorize each task into one of the four quadrants. Once categorized, you can create a plan of action based on the priorities, ensuring that urgent and important tasks are completed first and that time is allocated to important but not urgent tasks for long-term success.

Sample Chart of Eisenhower Matrix

Eisenhower Matrix

[Topic, Title, or Goal]

	URGENT	**NOT URGENT**

Do Immediately

☐ Example Task
☑ Example Task

PLAN and prioritize

I M P O R T A N T

DELEGATE for completion

DELETE these tasks

N O T

I M P O R T A N T

2. **Create a To-Do List**

Transfer the smaller tasks onto a to-do list or a task management tool. Writing down the tasks not only helps you visualize your progress but also provides a tangible record of what needs to be accomplished. Break each task down into actionable steps, making them as specific and clear as possible.

3. **Schedule Tasks Strategically**

Allocate specific intervals in your schedule to each task. Consider your energy levels, concentration abilities, and other commitments when assigning time for each task. Determine whether certain tasks require more focus and allocate your most productive hours accordingly. Strive for a balanced distribution of tasks throughout your day or week, ensuring that you don't overload yourself with too many complex tasks at once.

4. Use Time Blocking

Time blocking is a technique that involves dedicating specific blocks of time for specific tasks or types of activities. Assign dedicated blocks for focused work, such as studying, writing, or problem-solving. Protect these time blocks from distractions and interruptions, allowing yourself to immerse fully in the task at hand. Time blocking helps create structure, eliminates decision fatigue, and enhances productivity.

5. Employ the Pomodoro Technique

The Pomodoro Technique is a time management method that involves working in focused bursts of activity followed by short breaks.

Set a timer for a specific duration (e.g., 25 minutes), work intently on a task during that time, and then take a short break (e.g., 5 minutes). Repeat this cycle a few times before taking a longer break.

The Pomodoro Technique helps maintain focus, prevents burnout, and increases productivity.

Sample Chart of Pomodoro

POMODORO
DAILY PLANNER

DATE _____

PRODUCTIVITY
RATING

TODAY'S PRIORITY
What must you complete to feel a sense of accomplishment?

1. _____

○ ○○○○○○
Estimate   Pomodoro sessions completed

ADDITIONAL TASKS
List your remaining tasks in order of priority.

2. _____   ○ ○○○○○○
3. _____   ○ ○○○○○○
4. _____   ○ ○○○○○○
5. _____   ○ ○○○○○○
6. _____   ○ ○○○○○○
7. _____   ○ ○○○○○○
8. _____   ○ ○○○○○○

NOTES

BREAK IDEAS/TASKS

PRODUCTIVITY REVIEW
What will you improve tomorrow?

Twilights Publications

CHECKLIST
GOOD VIBES AHEAD
DATE _____

To stay motivated, you need to see some progress. So, break your main goal down into a list of smaller tasks so you can take smaller steps to see progress and check them off every day you do them. Good luck!

GOAL
My goal this week is _____

TASKS

	M	T	W	T	F	S	S
_____	○	○	○	○	○	○	○
_____	○	○	○	○	○	○	○
_____	○	○	○	○	○	○	○
_____	○	○	○	○	○	○	○
_____	○	○	○	○	○	○	○
_____	○	○	○	○	○	○	○
_____	○	○	○	○	○	○	○
_____	○	○	○	○	○	○	○
_____	○	○	○	○	○	○	○
_____	○	○	○	○	○	○	○
_____	○	○	○	○	○	○	○

WEEKLY REVIEW
How did you go this week? What will you improve next week?

_____
_____
_____
_____

DAILY PRODUCTIVITY METRICS

So you can keep track of how each productivity method is working for you throughout the week, we have created a quick rating system to measure your progress at the end of each day. Use it like this.

1. Read the statement.
2. Check the circle above the statement that best corresponds to your progress
3. Rate your overall mood by circling the face that best matches your feels.

WEDNESDAY

	NOT VERY		SOMEWHAT		VERY
I feel satisfied with my day.	○	○	○	○	○
I felt motivated.	○	○	○	○	○
I was productive.	○	○	○	○	○
I managed distractions well.	○	○	○	○	○
I feel balanced.	○	○	○	○	○
I made progress.	○	○	○	○	○

RATE YOUR MOOD

MONDAY

	NOT VERY		SOMEWHAT		VERY
I feel satisfied with my day.	○	○	○	○	○
I felt motivated.	○	○	○	○	○
I was productive.	○	○	○	○	○
I managed distractions well.	○	○	○	○	○
I feel balanced.	○	○	○	○	○
I made progress.	○	○	○	○	○

RATE YOUR MOOD

THURSDAY

	NOT VERY		SOMEWHAT		VERY
I feel satisfied with my day.	○	○	○	○	○
I felt motivated.	○	○	○	○	○
I was productive.	○	○	○	○	○
I managed distractions well.	○	○	○	○	○
I feel balanced.	○	○	○	○	○
I made progress.	○	○	○	○	○

RATE YOUR MOOD

TUESDAY

	NOT VERY		SOMEWHAT		VERY
I feel satisfied with my day.	○	○	○	○	○
I felt motivated.	○	○	○	○	○
I was productive.	○	○	○	○	○
I managed distractions well.	○	○	○	○	○
I feel balanced.	○	○	○	○	○
I made progress.	○	○	○	○	○

RATE YOUR MOOD

FRIDAY

	NOT VERY		SOMEWHAT		VERY
I feel satisfied with my day.	○	○	○	○	○
I felt motivated.	○	○	○	○	○
I was productive.	○	○	○	○	○
I managed distractions well.	○	○	○	○	○
I feel balanced.	○	○	○	○	○
I made progress.	○	○	○	○	○

RATE YOUR MOOD

Steps to Achieve Breaking Tasks into Manageable Chunks

Identify a Complex Task and Break It Down

Start by identifying a complex task or project that you need to accomplish. This could be a research paper, a coding project, a presentation, or any other assignment that feels overwhelming. Once you have identified the task, take a moment to analyse its requirements and structure. Break it down into smaller, actionable steps or milestones.

Ask yourself:

1. What are the key components or stages involved?
2. What are the specific actions or subtasks required to complete each component?

By breaking the task into manageable chunks, you create a roadmap that guides your progress and makes the overall task more approachable.

For example, if you have a research paper to complete, the breakdown could include steps such as conducting research, creating an outline, writing the introduction, body paragraphs, and conclusion, editing and revising, and finalizing the paper.

Allocate Time for Each Step in Your Schedule

Once you have identified the smaller steps or milestones, allocate dedicated time for each one in your schedule. Consider your existing commitments, deadlines, and the complexity of each task when determining the time required. Be realistic in your estimations and give yourself enough time to complete each step without feeling rushed or overwhelmed. Block out specific time slots in your schedule for each task, treating them as important appointments with yourself. By allocating time for each step, you ensure that you have a clear plan and a designated space for making progress.

For example, if you have allocated three hours for conducting research, mark it in your schedule and commit to utilizing that time solely for research-related activities. Similarly, allocate separate time slots for writing different sections of the paper, editing, and revising.

Celebrate Your Progress as You Complete Each Smaller Task

As you complete each smaller task or milestone, take a moment to acknowledge and celebrate your progress. Recognize the effort and dedication you put into accomplishing each step.

Celebrating your progress serves as a source of motivation and reinforces a positive mindset. It boosts your confidence and encourages you to continue moving forward. Celebrations can take various forms, depending on your preferences.

It could be as simple as taking a short break, treating yourself to a small reward, or sharing your achievements with a supportive friend or family member.

The key is to recognize and appreciate the progress you have made, no matter how small it may seem.

For instance, after completing the research phase of your project, you can reward yourself with a short walk outside or indulge in a favourite snack.

Similarly, after finishing each section of your research paper, take a moment to reflect on your accomplishment and share your progress with someone who understands the effort you have invested.

By following these actionable steps, you can effectively break down complex tasks into manageable chunks, allocate time for each step in your schedule, and celebrate your progress along the way.

This approach enables you to approach tasks with clarity, focus, and a sense of accomplishment, making your journey toward completion smoother and more rewarding.

Remember, each small step brings you closer to the ultimate goal, and by breaking tasks into manageable chunks, you harness the power of progress and propel yourself toward success in your college journey.

Finally, Breaking tasks into manageable chunks is a game-changer when it comes to effective time management. By understanding the concept of task breakdown and employing techniques to organize and schedule smaller tasks effectively, you can overcome the overwhelm of complex tasks and achieve greater productivity and success in college.

Remember, Rome wasn't built in a day, and neither are major tasks or projects. Embrace the power of task breakdown as a valuable tool in your time management arsenal. Take one step at a time, celebrate your progress along the way, and watch as the smaller tasks add up to significant achievements.

Overcoming Procrastination

"Don't wait. The time will never be just right."

- Napoleon Hill -

Procrastination—a formidable foe that plagues college students worldwide. It stealthily creeps into our lives, tempting us to put off important tasks until the last minute, and leaves us grappling with stress, anxiety, and subpar results. But fear not, dear reader, for within the pages of this chapter lies the antidote to this common time management challenge. In **"Overcoming Procrastination,"** we will unravel the mysteries behind this self-sabotaging behaviour, equip you with the tools to recognize its signs, and provide effective strategies to conquer it. Prepare to be empowered to break free from the clutches of procrastination and unleash your true potential.

Understanding the Reasons Behind Procrastination

Procrastination is when a person delays or puts off doing a task or activity that needs to be done. Instead of starting the task right away, they choose to do something else or postpone it until later. Procrastination often happens when a person feels unmotivated, overwhelmed, or unsure about how to begin the task. It can lead to increased stress and anxiety, as well as a sense of guilt or regret for not taking action earlier.

To overcome procrastination, we must first understand its roots. Procrastination often stems from a combination of internal and external factors. Internally, *fear of failure, perfectionism, lack of motivation, and feelings of being overwhelmed* can paralyze our ability to take action. Externally, *distractions, lack of structure, and poor time management skills* can contribute to our tendency to delay tasks. By delving into the underlying causes of procrastination, we can gain insights into our own behaviours and develop targeted strategies to combat it.

Recognizing the Signs of Procrastination

Procrastination can be a sneaky adversary, disguising itself in various forms. It's crucial to recognize the signs and catch ourselves in the act.

Some common indicators of procrastination include:

Delaying: Constantly postponing tasks and convincing ourselves that there is always time later.

Perfectionism: Setting impossibly high standards, leading to hesitation and avoidance of tasks.

Distractions: Engaging in activities that divert our attention from the task at hand, such as scrolling through social media or watching videos.

Rationalization: Justifying our delay with excuses like *"I work better under pressure"* or *"I'll do it when I feel more inspired."*

Task Switching: Jumping from one task to another without completing anything, creating a false sense of productivity.

Overplanning: Spending excessive time planning and organizing, often as a means of avoiding the actual work.

By familiarizing ourselves with these signs, we can interrupt the procrastination cycle and redirect our focus towards productive action.

Examples of Student Procrastination

Let me share some examples of student procrastination, which many of us can identify with. These stories highlight the struggles and consequences of delaying important tasks, showcasing the need for effective time management and self-discipline.

Example 1: *Imagine a student who has a pile of homework waiting for them. Instead of diving into the assignments, they spend the entire day surfing the internet, watching funny videos, and scrolling through social media. As the sun sets, they finally muster the motivation to start their work, regretting their wasted hours and wishing they had used their time more wisely.*

Example 2: *Consider a university student who has a crucial test approaching. Instead of hitting the books, they find themselves captivated by social media platforms, mindlessly scrolling through feeds, and getting lost in the virtual world. As the clock ticks away, panic sets in, and they cram for the exam at the* last minute, filled with regret for not starting their preparation earlier.

Example 3: Now picture a graduate student working on a major research project or dissertation. Despite the importance of the task, they constantly find reasons to delay working on it. They occupy themselves with trivial tasks, convincing themselves that they need to complete those first. As weeks turn into months, they realize the magnitude of their procrastination and the mountain of work that awaits them, feeling a sense of disappointment and frustration.

In addition to academic tasks, students can also procrastinate on other aspects of their lives.

Take the case of a student who wants to maintain a healthy lifestyle but continually puts off exercising. They convince themselves that they will start *tomorrow or that they are too busy with other obligations. Days turn into weeks, and their fitness goals remain untouched, leaving them feeling unsatisfied and yearning for change.*

These examples shed light on the common traps of student procrastination, highlighting the negative impact it can have on our academic performance, personal growth, and overall well-being. However, there is hope.

Strategies to Overcome Procrastination and Increase Productivity

Now that we have laid the foundation by understanding the reasons behind procrastination and recognizing its signs, it's time to equip ourselves with practical strategies to overcome it.

Here are some effective techniques to increase productivity and conquer procrastination:

Set Clear Goals and Deadlines:

Clearly define your goals and establish specific deadlines for each task. Breaking down larger goals into smaller, manageable tasks provides a sense of structure and creates a roadmap for progress. Set realistic deadlines that hold you accountable and foster a sense of urgency to get started.

Use the "Just Start" Technique:

One of the most challenging aspects of overcoming procrastination is taking the initial step.

The "just start" technique encourages you to commit to working on a task for just a few minutes. Once you get started, the momentum often builds, and it becomes easier to continue working. The key is to overcome the inertia and take that first small step forward.

Utilize Time Blocking:

Time blocking involves scheduling blocks of time dedicated to specific tasks or activities. Allocate focused periods for studying, working on assignments, and engaging in other important activities. By establishing a structured routine, you create a sense of discipline and prioritize your tasks effectively.

Break Your Tasks Down into Smaller Chunks

Remember the importance of breaking tasks into manageable chunks, as discussed in Chapter 3. When faced with a daunting task, divide it into smaller, more achievable subtasks. This not only makes the task feel less overwhelming but also provides a sense of progress and accomplishment as you complete each subtask.

Find Your Optimal Working Environment:

Identify the environment that best supports your focus and productivity. Experiment with different settings, whether it's studying in the library, a quiet café, or a designated study space at home. Discover the conditions that minimize distractions and help you enter a state of flow, where your productivity soars.

Practice the Pomodoro Technique:

The Pomodoro Technique is a time management technique that involves taking short breaks after working hard. Set a timer for a predetermined period, such as 25 minutes, and work on a task with full concentration. When the timer goes off, take a short break of around five minutes. Repeat this cycle three or four times, and after completing a few cycles, reward yourself with a longer break.

This technique enhances productivity by capitalizing on focused work intervals and allowing for rejuvenating breaks.

Seek Accountability and Support:

Enlist the support of a study buddy, a mentor, or a friend who shares similar goals. Being accountable to someone can provide motivation and help you stay on track. Regular check-ins and shared progress can foster a sense of community and encourage each other to overcome procrastination.

Case Studies and Success Stories:

To further illustrate the effectiveness of the strategies discussed in this chapter, let's explore a few case studies and success stories of individuals who have overcome procrastination and achieved remarkable results.

Case Study 1: *Sarah, a college student struggling with procrastination, implemented the strategies* outlined in this chapter. By breaking down her assignments, setting specific deadlines, and utilizing time blocking, she transformed her approach to studying. Sarah experienced a significant increase in productivity, reduced stress levels, and improved grades.

Success Story 1: *Jason, a graduate student, recognized that his procrastination was rooted in perfectionism. Through self-reflection and practicing the **"just start"** technique, he learned to embrace imperfect action and gradually overcame his fear of failure. This newfound mindset empowered Jason to complete his thesis ahead of schedule and earn accolades for his research.*

Success Story 2: *Emily, an overwhelmed college student juggling multiple responsibilities, struggled to prioritize her tasks effectively. By adopting the* **Pomodoro Technique** *and breaking down her to-do list into smaller chunks, she regained control over her time. Emily's newfound ability to organize and schedule tasks allowed her to excel academically while maintaining a healthy work-life balance.*

Procrastination is a formidable opponent that can hinder our academic and personal growth. By understanding its underlying causes, recognizing its signs, and employing effective strategies, we can conquer procrastination and unlock our true potential.

Actionable Steps to Overcome Procrastination

Identify Your Personal Procrastination Triggers and Develop Strategies to Counter Them.

1. Start by reflecting on your own patterns of procrastination.
2. Identify the specific triggers that often lead you to delay tasks or engage in unproductive activities.
3. It could be fear of failure, perfectionism, lack of motivation, or even external distractions.

Once you have identified your triggers, develop strategies to counteract them.

For example: If fear of failure holds you back, remind yourself that mistakes and setbacks are a natural part of the learning process. Adopt a growth mindset and focus on progress rather than perfection.

If external distractions like social media or your phone divert your attention, consider implementing techniques such as blocking specific websites during study sessions or using productivity apps that limit your access to distracting apps.

If lack of motivation is an issue, find ways to tap into your intrinsic motivation by connecting the task at hand to your personal goals and values. Visualize the benefits of completing the task and remind yourself of the sense of accomplishment that comes with it.

Use time blocking techniques to allocate specific time to important tasks:

Time blocking is a powerful technique to combat procrastination and increase productivity. Start by creating a schedule or calendar that outlines your day, allocating specific time blocks for important tasks. When planning your schedule, consider your **peak energy levels** and identify the periods when you are most focused and productive. Dedicate these prime hours to tackling challenging or high-priority tasks. Be realistic in estimating the time required for each task and avoid overcommitting yourself. By assigning dedicated time blocks, you create a sense of structure and accountability, ensuring that important tasks are given the attention they deserve.

Practice the *"Five-Minute Rule"* to Get Started on a Task, even if it Feels Overwhelming:

The hardest part of overcoming procrastination is often getting started. To overcome this initial resistance, employ the "five-minute rule." The rule is simple: commit to working on a task for just five minutes, regardless of how daunting it may seem. Set a timer and dive into the task with focused effort for those five minutes. More often than not, you'll find that once you overcome the initial inertia, you gain momentum and can continue working for an extended period. The key is to overcome the psychological barrier of starting and leverage the power of small, consistent actions. Even if you end up stopping after five minutes, you would have made some progress and overcome the mental resistance associated with starting.

Remember that overcoming procrastination is an ongoing process that requires self-awareness, discipline, and consistent effort. Be kind to yourself and celebrate the small accomplishments along the way. By identifying your triggers, implementing time-blocking techniques, and practicing the five-minute rule, you'll develop resilience against procrastination and empower yourself to take decisive action towards your goals. Embrace the power of intentional action and watch as your productivity soars, and your accomplishments multiply.

Managing Distractions

"Time is what we want most, but what

we use worst."

- William Penn -

Distractions are abundant and can pose a significant challenge to effective time management, especially for college students. The ability to maintain focus amidst a sea of distractions is a valuable skill that can greatly enhance productivity and academic success.

Common Distractions Faced by Students

As a college student, you find yourself constantly bombarded with distractions that can derail your concentration and hinder your progress. Some common distractions include:

Social Media: The allure of social media platforms, such as Facebook, Instagram, and Twitter, can easily consume hours of your time if left unchecked. The constant notifications, messages, and the desire to stay connected with friends can pull your attention away from important tasks.

Technology: While technology has many benefits, it can also be a double-edged sword when it comes to distractions. Mobile phones, tablets, and laptops provide access to endless sources of entertainment and information, making it challenging to resist the temptation to browse, stream videos, or play games.

Noisy Environments: Living in dorms or shared spaces can expose you to constant noise and interruptions, making it difficult to concentrate on your studies. Roommates, loud neighbours, or bustling common areas can disrupt your focus and hinder productivity.

Procrastination: Procrastination itself is a significant distraction. It is the art of finding alternative activities to avoid the tasks at hand. Engaging in non-productive activities or delaying important responsibilities can waste valuable time and lead to increased stress levels.

Creating a Conducive Study Environment

To effectively manage distractions, it is crucial to create a study environment that promotes focus and productivity. Consider the following strategies:

Designate a Dedicated Study Space: Set aside a specific area in your living space that is solely dedicated to studying. This could be a desk, a quiet corner, or a designated study room. Having a consistent study space helps signal your brain that it's time to focus and minimizes external interruptions.

Minimize Noise: Identify the noise sources in your environment and take steps to minimize them. Use noise-cancelling headphones, play ambient background music, or explore quiet study areas on campus or in the library.

Alternatively, you can try using white noise or nature sounds to create a calm and focused atmosphere.

Remove Temptations: Keep distractions out of sight and out of reach. Put your mobile phone on silent mode or place it in another room while studying. Install website blockers or apps that limit your access to distracting websites or social media platforms during study sessions.

Establish Boundaries: Communicate with roommates, friends, and family members about your study schedule and the importance of uninterrupted study time. Set clear boundaries and ask for their cooperation in minimizing distractions during your designated study periods.

Techniques to Minimize Distractions and Maintain Focus

Now that you have set up a conducive study environment, it's time to implement techniques to minimize distractions and maintain unwavering focus. Here are some effective strategies:

Time Blocking: Incorporate time-blocking techniques into your schedule. Allocate specific time blocks for focused studying and designate specific time slots for checking emails, social media, or engaging in leisure activities. By creating designated periods for distractions, you can maintain better control over their influence on your study time.

Pomodoro Technique: The Pomodoro Technique is a time management method that involves dividing your study sessions into targeted periods of time, usually 25 minutes, followed by short breaks. This technique helps maintain concentration and provides regular intervals for relaxation and recharging.

Practice Mindfulness: Cultivate mindfulness during your study sessions. Focus on the present moment, acknowledging distractions without getting caught up in them. Train your mind to return to the task at hand whenever you notice your attention drifting.

Prioritize Tasks: Determine the most important tasks that require your immediate attention and focus. Rank them based on their significance and allocate your peak focus hours to tackle them. By prioritizing tasks, you can ensure that essential responsibilities are addressed first, reducing the stress caused by unfinished tasks looming over your head.

Managing distractions is a crucial aspect of effective time management for college students. By understanding the common distractions faced, creating a conducive study environment, and implementing techniques to minimize distractions and maintain focus, you can significantly enhance your productivity and achieve academic success.

Steps to Achieve "Managing Distractions".

Identify Your Biggest Distractions and Find Ways to Limit Their Influence:

1. Take some time to reflect on the distractions that tend to disrupt your focus the most. Is it

social media, your mobile phone, noisy environments, or something else?

2. Once you have identified your biggest distractions, brainstorm strategies to limit their influence. For example, if social media is a major distraction, consider setting specific times for checking it rather than mindlessly scrolling throughout the day.

3. Try out with different methods to find what works best for you. This could include turning off notifications, using the **"Do Not Disturb"** mode on your phone, or temporarily disabling certain apps during study sessions.

Designate A Quiet Study Space and Eliminate Potential Distractions from That Area

1. Choose a study space that is quiet and conducive to concentration. This could be a library, a quiet corner in your home, or a study room on campus.

2. Clear the study area of any potential distractions. Remove or hide items that may tempt you to engage in non-study-related activities. Keep your workspace clean and organized to promote a focused mindset.

3. Communicate with those around you, such as roommates or family members, about the importance of maintaining a quiet environment during your designated study times.

Use Apps or Browser Extensions to Block Distracting Websites or Notifications During Study Time

1. Explore the various productivity apps or browser extensions available that can help you block or limit access to distracting websites or apps.

   Examples include StayFocusd, Freedom, or RescueTime.

2. Set up specific time blocks during which these apps or extensions will restrict access to distracting websites or temporarily disable notifications on your devices.

3. Experiment with different settings to find the level of restriction that works best for you. Gradually increase the intensity of the

restrictions if you find that you are still easily tempted by distractions.

Managing distractions is a crucial skill to develop in order to maximize your time and productivity as a college student. By taking actionable steps to identify and limit your biggest distractions, designating a quiet study space, and utilizing apps or browser extensions to block distractions, you can create an environment that supports focused and effective studying. Remember, it's important to find the strategies that work best for you and be consistent in implementing them. With dedication and perseverance, you can overcome distractions and maintain the focus necessary to achieve your academic goals. Stay committed, adapt as needed, and let your determination guide you towards success.

Efficient Study Techniques

"Success is the sum of small efforts, repeated

day in and day out."

- Robert Collier -

In the journey of academic excellence, effective studying holds the key to unlocking your true potential. It is the cornerstone upon which your knowledge is built and your accomplishments are achieved. As a college student, you are faced with the challenge of managing multiple subjects, assignments, and exams. The ability to study efficiently not only saves you time but also enhances your comprehension and retention of information. In this chapter, we will explore a multitude of strategies, techniques, and resources to help you become a master of efficient studying. Get ready to embark on a transformative journey that will revolutionize the way you approach your academic endeavours.

Strategies for Effective Studying

Create a Study Plan: The first step towards efficient studying is to create a well-structured study plan. Break down your subjects into manageable chunks and allocate specific time slots for each. This allows for focused studying and ensures that you cover all the necessary topics.

Practice Active Learning: Passive reading can be ineffective in retaining information. Instead, engage in active learning techniques such as summarizing, questioning, and discussing concepts. This not only deepens your understanding but also helps you to actively engage with the material.

Utilize the Pomodoro Technique: The Pomodoro Technique is a time management method that involves studying for a focused period of time (typically 25 minutes) followed by a short break. This technique helps to maintain concentration and prevent burnout.

Take regular breaks: Studying for long periods without breaks can lead to diminished results. It is important to take regular breaks to rest and recharge your mind. Use these breaks to engage in activities that relax and rejuvenate you, such as going for a walk or practicing mindfulness.

Maximizing Concentration and Retention

Create a distraction-free environment: Find a quiet, well-lit study space where you can minimize distractions. Turn off notifications on your phone or use apps that block annoying websites. Clear your study area of clutter and create a conducive environment that promotes focus and concentration.

Use Effective Note-Taking Techniques: Develop a note-taking system that works best for you. Whether it's using bullet points, mind maps, or Cornell note-taking, find a method that enhances your understanding and allows for easy review. Reviewing your notes regularly helps reinforce your learning and improves retention.

Practice Spaced Repetition: Spaced repetition is a technique that involves reviewing information at increasing intervals over time. Instead of cramming all the information at once, spaced repetition allows for better retention and long-term memory.

Engage in Active Recall: Instead of simply re-reading your notes, actively retrieve information from memory. Test yourself with practice questions, quizzes, or flashcards. This helps reinforce your learning and identifies areas that need further review.

Utilizing Study Resources and Tools

Leverage Online Resources: Take advantage of the abundance of online study resources available. Access educational websites, online courses, and video tutorials that provide additional explanations and practice materials. These resources can supplement your learning and provide alternative perspectives on complex topics.

Form Study Groups: Collaborating with fellow students can be highly beneficial. Join or form study groups where you can discuss and review material together. Explaining concepts to others not only reinforces your understanding but also exposes you to different viewpoints.

Utilize Technology Tools: Various technology tools can enhance your studying experience. Use note-taking apps, productivity apps, and flashcard applications to streamline your studying process. Online research databases and citation management tools can also assist in organizing your academic resources.

Seek Help from Academic Support Services: If you find yourself struggling with a particular subject, don't hesitate to seek help from academic support services. Most colleges offer tutoring programs, writing centres, and study skills workshops that can provide guidance and assistance tailored to your needs.

Actionable Steps for Managing Distractions

Explore different study techniques and find the ones that work best for you:

Experiment with different study techniques to discover what helps you stay focused and engaged. Some popular techniques include the **Pomodoro Technique,** the **Feynman Technique**, and the **SQ3R Method.**

Try using visual aids, such as diagrams, mind maps, or flashcards, to enhance your understanding and retention of information.

Utilize mnemonic devices or memory techniques to help you remember key concepts or information.

Divide your study session into manageable units with short breaks in between:

Break your study time into smaller, more focused sessions.

For example, study for 25 minutes and then take a 5-minute break. This approach, known as the Pomodoro Technique, helps prevent mental fatigue and improves concentration.

During your breaks, engage in activities that help you relax and recharge, such as stretching, going for a short walk, or practicing deep breathing exercises.

Use a timer or a productivity app to keep track of your study and break intervals, ensuring that you stick to the planned schedule.

Take advantage of resources such as textbooks, online materials, and study groups:

Textbooks: Utilize your textbooks as primary sources of information. Develop effective reading strategies, such as skimming, scanning, and highlighting relevant information.

Online materials: Take advantage of online resources, such as lecture notes, video tutorials, educational websites, and interactive quizzes. These resources can supplement your understanding and provide alternative explanations.

Study groups: Join or form study groups with classmates who are committed to academic success. Collaborating with others can help you stay motivated, gain different perspectives, and share knowledge. Discussing challenging concepts or solving problems together can enhance your learning experience.

Seek guidance from professors, teaching assistants, or academic support services if you encounter difficulties or need clarification on specific topics.

Remember, managing distractions requires self-discipline and a proactive approach. It's essential to create a study environment conducive to focus and minimize external interruptions. Additionally, developing effective time management skills and prioritizing tasks can also contribute to reducing distractions and increasing productivity. With consistent practice and a commitment to your academic goals, you will gain the ability to manage distractions effectively and optimize your study sessions for maximum success

Self-Care and Time for Relaxation

"Taking care of yourself is not a luxury; it's a necessity."

- Unknown –

I n the hustle and bustle of college life, it's easy to get caught up in the whirlwind of academic responsibilities, extracurricular activities, and social engagements. The constant demands on your time can leave you feeling overwhelmed, stressed, and burned out. However, amidst the chaos, it is crucial to remember that self-care is not a luxury but a necessity. It is the foundation upon which effective time management and overall well-being are built.

The Importance of Self-Care in Time Management

Self-care is the practice of nurturing your physical, mental, and emotional well-being. It involves taking deliberate actions to prioritize your needs, recharge your energy, and maintain a healthy work-life balance. While it may seem counterintuitive to allocate time for self-care when your schedule is already packed, neglecting it can lead to diminished productivity, decreased motivation, and compromised health.

By incorporating self-care into your time management strategy, you invest in your overall well-being, which in turn enhances your ability to manage time effectively. It allows you to approach your academic responsibilities with clarity, focus, and renewed energy. Self-care empowers you to show up as your best self, both in your studies and in other areas of your life.

Balancing Academic Responsibilities with Personal Well-Being

Achieving a healthy balance between academic responsibilities and personal well-being is crucial for long-term success and fulfilment. It's essential to recognize that your worth is not solely determined by your academic achievements. Taking care of your physical, mental, and emotional health is equally important.

Here are some strategies for striking a balance between academic responsibilities and personal well-being:

Prioritize Self-Care: Make self-care a Priority in your daily routine. Schedule time for activities that bring you joy and relaxation, such as exercise, hobbies, spending time with loved ones, or practicing mindfulness and meditation.

Set boundaries: Learn to say no to excessive commitments that may compromise your well-being. Establish clear boundaries around your time and energy, ensuring you have enough space for self-care and relaxation.

Practice time management techniques: Utilize the time management techniques outlined in this book to optimize your productivity and create more time for self-care. By effectively managing your tasks and setting realistic goals, you can reduce stress and free up time for activities that replenish your energy.

Incorporating Relaxation and Downtime into Your Routine

Relaxation and downtime are essential components of a well-rounded and fulfilling college experience. They provide an opportunity for rest, rejuvenation, and mental recharge. By deliberately carving out time for relaxation, you can enhance your overall well-being and maintain a sustainable approach to time management.

Consider the following strategies for incorporating relaxation and downtime into your routine:

Unplug from technology: Set aside designated periods of time where you disconnect from digital devices and engage in activities that promote relaxation, such as reading a book, going for a nature walk, or engaging in creative pursuits.

Practice mindfulness and meditation: Cultivate mindfulness through practices such as meditation, deep breathing exercises, or yoga. These practices help calm the mind, reduce stress, and increase focus and clarity.

Engage in hobbies and passions: Dedicate time to activities that bring you joy and fulfilment. Whether it's playing a musical instrument, painting, writing, or playing a sport, engaging in hobbies allows you to recharge and tap into your creative side.

Prioritize quality sleep: Ensure that you prioritize sufficient and restful sleep. Create a bedtime routine, establish a comfortable sleep environment, and aim for a consistent sleep schedule. Quality sleep rejuvenates your body and mind, enhancing your overall well-being and productivity.

Specific Steps to Achieve "Self-Care and Time for Relaxation"

Prioritize self-care activities such as exercise, hobbies, and time with loved ones:

Make a list of self-care activities that bring you joy and rejuvenation. This could include activities like going for a walk, practicing yoga, reading a book, listening to music, or engaging in a hobby you enjoy.

Allocate specific time slots in your schedule dedicated to these activities. Treat them as non-negotiable appointments with yourself and give them the same level of importance as your academic commitments.

Involve your loved ones in your self-care routine. Spend quality time with friends and family, engage in meaningful conversations, and create memories together. Social connections can contribute to your overall well-being and provide support during stressful times.

Schedule regular breaks and relaxation time in your daily routine:

Recognize the importance of breaks in maintaining focus and productivity. Plan short breaks throughout your study or work sessions to rest and recharge.

Experiment with different activities and breaks to find what works best for you. Some people find that short, frequent breaks every 25-30 minutes work well, while others prefer longer breaks every 60-90 minutes.

Use your breaks to engage in activities that promote relaxation and rejuvenation. Stretch, take a walk, listen to music, or engage in a mindfulness exercise to clear your mind and recharge your energy.

Practice stress management techniques, such as deep breathing or meditation, during busy periods:

Stress is an inevitable part of college life, but how you manage it can make a significant difference in your well-being. Incorporate stress management techniques into your routine to help you navigate challenging periods.

Deep breathing exercises can be done anywhere and anytime, providing an instant calming effect. Take a few deep breaths through your nose, hold them for a moment, and then gently let them out through your lips. Repeat this process several times to relieve tension and promote relaxation.

Explore mindfulness and meditation practices. Take a few minutes each day to sit quietly, focus on your breathing, and observe your thoughts without judgment. This practice cultivates present-moment awareness and helps reduce stress.

Consider incorporating other stress-reducing activities into your routine, such as journaling, practicing gratitude, or engaging in gentle physical exercises like yoga or tai chi.

Remember, self-care is not a luxury but a necessity for your overall well-being and academic success. By prioritizing self-care activities, scheduling regular breaks and relaxation time, and practicing stress management techniques, you create a balanced and sustainable approach to time management. Embrace these actionable steps and make self-care a priority in your college journey.

Strategies for Time Management during Exams

"The key is not to prioritize what's on your schedule, but to schedule your priorities."

- Stephen Covey –

Exams are an inevitable part of the college experience, and effective time management during this critical period can make a significant difference in your academic performance. In this chapter, we will delve into strategies for time management during exams, helping you develop effective exam preparation plans and providing tips for managing your time on exam days. By implementing these techniques, you can approach exams with confidence, minimize stress, and maximize your chances of success.

Developing Effective Exam Preparation Plans

Effective exam preparation involves more than just cramming and last-minute studying. It requires a well-thought-out plan that allows you to cover the necessary material, reinforce key concepts, and build confidence.

Here are some key steps to develop an effective exam preparation plan:

1. Evaluate The Exam Content and Format:

Familiarize yourself with the exam structure, including the types of questions, time constraints, and weighting of different sections.

Understand the scope and depth of the material that will be covered in the exam. This will help you determine the amount of time and effort required for each topic.

2. Break Down the Material into Manageable Study Sessions:

Divide the material into smaller, manageable chunks based on topics or chapters. This approach allows you to allocate specific study sessions to cover each portion effectively.

Create a study schedule that includes dedicated time slots for each topic. This will help you stay organized and cover all the necessary content before the exam.

3. Prioritize And Allocate Study Time:

Identify the areas that require more attention or that you find more challenging. Allocate more study time to these topics to ensure a thorough understanding.

Balance your study sessions by incorporating regular breaks to avoid mental fatigue. Short, focused study periods followed by brief breaks can improve your overall productivity.

4. Utilize Active Learning Techniques:

Engage in active learning methods such as summarizing, teaching the material to someone else, or creating flashcards. These techniques promote active engagement, deep understanding, and retention of the material.

Form study groups with your classmates to discuss and review course material. Explaining concepts to others can improve your understanding and provide different perspectives.

Tips for Time Management during Exam Days

Effective time management on exam days is crucial to maintaining focus, managing stress, and performing at your best. Consider the following tips to make the most of your time during exams:

1. Start your day with a healthy routine:

Get a good night's sleep before the exam day to ensure optimal mental alertness and focus.

Begin your day with a nutritious breakfast to provide energy for the exam.

Arrive early and organize your exam materials:

Plan to arrive at the exam venue well before the scheduled time to avoid rushing and reduce stress.

Organize your exam materials, including pens, pencils, calculators, and any permitted reference materials, in advance.

2. Read And Understand the Instructions:

Take a few minutes to carefully read through the exam instructions before starting. Understand your requirements and allocate your time accordingly.

3. Manage Your Time Effectively During the Exam:

Allocate time for each section or question based on their weight and complexity. This will help you prioritize your efforts and ensure that you complete all the required tasks within the given time.

If you come across a difficult question, go ahead and come back to it later. Managing your time strategically will prevent you from getting stuck on a single question and running out of time for the rest of the exam.

4. Stay Focused and Maintain a Positive Mindset:

Keep distractions at bay and stay fully engaged in the exam. Remember your preparation and believe in your abilities.

If you find yourself feeling anxious or overwhelmed during the exam, take a deep breath, relax, and regain your focus. Positive self-talk can help boost your confidence and concentration.

5. Review your answers:

Take your time to check your answers at the end of the test. Use this opportunity to check for any errors or incomplete responses.

Be cautious not to spend too much time on review, as it may cause unnecessary stress and eat into the overall exam time.

Effective time management during exams is a skill that can significantly impact your academic performance. By developing effective exam preparation plans and implementing time management strategies on exam days, you can optimize your performance, reduce stress, and achieve the results you desire.

Specific Steps

1. Create a study schedule specifically tailored for exams:

Evaluate the exam dates and prioritize them based on their proximity and importance.

Identify the subjects or topics that require more attention and allocate more study time to them.

Break down your study schedule into manageable study sessions. Aim for shorter, focused study periods rather than long, unproductive cramming sessions.

Consider your personal preferences and energy levels when scheduling study sessions. Some individuals perform better in the morning, while others are more productive in the evening. Align your study schedule with your peak concentration times.

2. Break down your study material into manageable chunks:

Divide your study material into smaller, manageable chunks based on topics or sub-topics. Breaking down complex subjects into smaller parts helps you approach them more effectively.

Create a study plan that outlines which topics you will cover in each study session. This way, you can track your progress and ensure that you cover all the necessary content before the exam.

Prioritize challenging or unfamiliar topics, but also allocate time for revision and review of previously covered material. Balancing new learning with reinforcement is crucial for retention and understanding.

3. Utilize techniques like practice exams and active review to optimize study time:

Practice exams are invaluable tools for exam preparation. Obtain past exam papers or practice questions relevant to your subjects and attempt them under exam conditions. This helps you become familiar with the exam format and identify areas that require further attention.

Engage in active review techniques such as summarizing, teaching the material to someone else, or creating flashcards. These techniques promote active engagement with the material, enhance understanding, and improve retention.

Consider forming study groups with classmates to discuss and review course material together. Sharing perspectives and teaching others can deepen your understanding and provide valuable insights.

Case Study: Emily's Exam Success Story.

Emily, a college student majoring in biology, was overwhelmed with her upcoming exams. She had a large amount of material to cover and was unsure how to manage her time effectively. However, by implementing the following strategies, Emily was able to navigate her exams with confidence:

Creating a study schedule tailored to her exams:

Emily identified her exam dates and allocated study time based on the proximity and importance of each exam. She scheduled study sessions for each subject, ensuring she had enough time to cover all the material.

Breaking down her study material:

Emily divided her biology textbook into chapters and assigned specific study sessions to each chapter. This approach allowed her to focus on one topic at a time and ensured she covered all the necessary content.

Utilizing practice exams and active review:

Emily found past exam papers and practice questions to test her understanding of the material. She simulated exam conditions and used the results to identify areas that needed improvement. Additionally, Emily actively reviewed the material by summarizing each chapter and teaching it to her study group.

Emily's dedication and strategic approach paid off, and she successfully passed her exams with flying colours.

Her story highlights the effectiveness of tailored study schedules, breaking down study material, and utilizing practice exams and active review techniques.

Conclusion:

Effective time management during exams is crucial for academic success. By creating a study schedule tailored to your exams, breaking down your study material, and utilizing techniques like practice exams and active review, you can optimize your study time and improve your understanding and document retention.

Remember, studying smarter, not harder, is the key to achieving your desired exam results. Embrace these strategies, stay focused, and approach your exams with confidence.

Embracing Time Management for Academic Success

"Time is a created thing. To say 'I don't have time,' is like saying, 'I don't want to.'"

- Lao Tzu -

Throughout this book, we have explored various effective time management techniques specifically tailored for college students. We have discovered the power of goal setting, the importance of prioritization, and the need to break tasks into manageable chunks. We have discussed strategies to overcome procrastination, manage distractions, and optimize study techniques. Now, as we near the end of our journey together, it is time to reflect on the transformative impact of effective time management on academic success and the ongoing commitment required to maintain these principles.

The Transformative Impact of Effective Time Management on Academic Success

Effective time management is not just a series of strategies and techniques; it is a **mindset** and a **way of life**. When implemented consistently, it has the power to transform your academic journey and pave the way for success. Here are some key ways in which effective time management can impact your academic pursuits:

1. Enhanced Productivity:

By effectively managing your time, you can maximize your productivity and accomplish more in less time.

Allocating dedicated time slots for studying, completing assignments, and engaging in other academic tasks allows you to make the most of your available resources.

2. Improved Focus and Concentration:

Time management techniques help you eliminate distractions, create a conducive study environment, and maintain focus on the task at hand. By minimizing interruptions and maintaining concentration, you can deepen your understanding of the subject matter and retain information more effectively.

3. Reduced Stress and Anxiety:

Effective time management reduces last-minute cramming and the pressure of impending deadlines, leading to reduced stress and anxiety levels.

By spreading out your workload and planning ahead, you can approach tasks with a calmer mindset and perform at your best.

4. Better Time Allocation for Self-Care:

Time management principles emphasize the importance of self-care and maintaining a healthy work-life balance.

By allocating time for relaxation, exercise, hobbies, and personal relationships, you can nurture your well-being, recharge your energy, and prevent burnout.

Reflecting on Your Journey and the Progress Made

As you near the end of this book, take a moment to reflect on your personal journey and the progress you have made in implementing effective time management techniques.

Consider the following questions:

1. How have you seen your time management skills evolve since the beginning of your college journey?

2. What specific strategies have you found most effective in optimizing your time and productivity?

3. Have you experienced any notable improvements in your academic performance, stress levels, or overall well-being as a result of implementing these techniques?

4. How have you adjusted your schedule and priorities to accommodate unforeseen challenges or changes?

Acknowledging the Ongoing Commitment to Time Management Principles

Effective time management is not a one-time effort but a continuous commitment. As you reflect on your journey, acknowledge the ongoing dedication and effort required to maintain time management principles.

Consider the following aspects:

Consistency:

Consistency is key in maintaining effective time management. It is essential to continue practicing the techniques and strategies outlined in this book to reap long-term benefits.

Regularly review your goals, priorities, and schedules to ensure they align with your current academic demands and personal aspirations.

Flexibility and Adaptability:

Recognize that circumstances may change, and your time management strategies may need to adapt accordingly.

Stay open to exploring new techniques, adjusting your routines, and seeking support when needed.

Celebrating the Positive Outcomes and Achievements Resulting from Effective Time Management

Take a moment to celebrate the positive outcomes and achievements resulting from your commitment to effective time management. Acknowledge the milestones you have reached and the progress you have made.

Here are some achievements worth celebrating:

Academic Milestones:

Recognize the improvements in your grades, performance on exams and assignments, and overall academic progress.

Celebrate the successful completion of projects, presentations, and coursework.

Personal Growth:

Acknowledge the personal growth you have experienced throughout your time management journey.

Celebrate your increased self-discipline, improved organization skills, and enhanced ability to balance multiple responsibilities.

Work-Life Balance:

Celebrate your ability to carve out time for self-care, hobbies, and spending quality time with loved ones while managing your academic commitments. Reflect on the improved work-life balance you have achieved.

Steps to Embrace Time Management for Academic Success

1. **Continuously Assess and Adjust Your Strategies as Needed:**

To truly embrace time management for academic success, it is crucial to continuously assess and adjust your strategies as needed.

Here are actionable steps to help you in this process:

i. Regularly evaluate your current strategies:

Take the time to reflect on your current time management techniques. Are they effective? Are there any areas that need improvement? Identifying what is working and what needs adjustment is the first step toward optimizing your approach.

ii. Stay open to trying new strategies:

Don't be afraid to explore different time management techniques. Attend workshops, read books, or consult with experts to discover new approaches that may resonate with you. Embrace a growth mindset that welcomes change and improvement.

iii. Fine-tune your system:

Be proactive in fine-tuning your time management system. Adjust your schedule, routines, and productivity tools to align with your evolving needs and circumstances. Remember, what worked for you in one semester may not work as well in another.

iv. Seek feedback:

Seek feedback from mentors, professors, or trusted peers who can provide insights on your time management practices. Their perspectives can offer valuable advice and help you identify blind spots or areas for improvement.

2. **Seek support and accountability from peers, mentors, or study groups**

Building a support system and cultivating accountability are essential for effective time management.

Here are actionable steps to seek support and accountability:

i.   Form study groups:

Join or create study groups with peers who share similar academic goals. Collaborating with others allows you to exchange ideas, share resources, and hold each other accountable for staying on track with your study schedules.

ii.   Find a mentor:

Seek guidance from mentors who have successfully navigated the challenges of time management. They can provide valuable insights, share their experiences, and offer advice tailored to your specific needs.

iii.   Leverage technology:

Use productivity apps or online platforms that facilitate accountability. Some tools allow you to share progress with others or set deadlines for specific tasks, ensuring that you stay committed to your time management goals.

iv.   Participate   in   time   management
    workshops or seminars:

Attend workshops or seminars focused on time management. These events often provide opportunities to connect with like-minded individuals and offer practical strategies for effective time management.

3. Stay motivated by reminding yourself of the benefits and rewards of effective time management

Motivation plays a vital role in sustaining effective time management habits.

Here are actionable steps to stay motivated:

i.   Reflect on the benefits:

Remind yourself of the positive outcomes and rewards of effective time management. This may include improved academic performance, reduced stress levels, increased free time for hobbies, or a sense of accomplishment.

ii.   Set specific goals:

Establish specific goals related to time management. Whether it's completing assignments ahead of schedule, maintaining a consistent study routine, or finding a healthy work-life balance, setting clear objectives will keep you focused and motivated.

iii.   Track your progress:

Use a journal or a tracking system to monitor your progress. Seeing the tangible evidence of your accomplishments can provide a sense of motivation and encouragement, especially during challenging times.

iv.   Celebrate milestones:

Celebrate the milestones you achieve along your time management journey. Treat yourself to small rewards when you accomplish your goals, reinforcing the positive outcomes and fostering a sense of fulfilment.

4. Embrace Time Management as A Lifelong Skill That Extends Beyond Your Academic Journey:

Time management is not just a skill for your college years; it is a lifelong tool for success.

Here are actionable steps to embrace time management beyond academia:

i.   Recognize the broader applications:

Understand that effective time management extends beyond academic pursuits. It is a skill that can benefit your personal life, professional career, and personal development.

ii.   Cultivate a growth mindset:

Embrace the mindset that time management is a continuous learning process. Be open to new strategies, adapt to changing circumstances, and seek opportunities to further develop your time management skills throughout your life.

iii.   Explore resources and professional development:

Continuously seek out resources, books, workshops, and online courses that can deepen your knowledge and refine your time management techniques. Stay engaged in lifelong learning to enhance your time management skills.

iv.   Share your knowledge:

As you master effective time management techniques, share your knowledge with others. Mentor fellow students, offer guidance to colleagues, or volunteer in organizations where you can contribute your expertise. Teaching others reinforces your own understanding and helps create a positive ripple effect.

Conclusion:

Embracing time management for academic success requires continuous assessment, seeking support, staying motivated, and recognizing its lifelong value. By taking these actionable steps, you can cultivate effective time management habits that will not only benefit your college journey but also extend far beyond, empowering you to achieve success in all aspects of your life. Remember, time management is not just a means to an end; it is a transformative tool that will accompany you throughout your academic journey and beyond.

NOTE

We sincerely hope you find value in *"Time Management Guide for College Students."* If this book resonates with you and you believe it can make a positive difference in the lives of others, we kindly ask for your support. By leaving a **REVIEW** and sharing your experience with friends, family, and fellow readers, you play a crucial role in spreading the message of effective time management and helping others discover the transformative benefits within these pages.

Your thoughtful feedback and word-of-mouth recommendations have the power to inspire and guide others towards a path of greater productivity and success.

We **deeply appreciate your support** in sharing the gift of effective time management with the world. Together, we can empower college students to overcome overwhelm and achieve their goals with confidence and ease.

Closing Remarks

"Congratulations! You have reached the end of 'Time Management Guide for College Students.' Throughout this journey, we have explored essential strategies and actionable steps to help you *Optimize your time, be more productive, and achieve academic success.*

But remember, time management is not just a checklist of tasks to complete—it is a mindset, a lifestyle, and a transformative tool that can unlock your full potential.

As you embark on your college journey and beyond, remember that effective time management is not about squeezing every minute out of your day or sacrificing your well-being. It's about finding the balance that works for you, prioritizing your goals, and making intentional choices that align with your values and aspirations.

There will be challenges along the way—distractions, procrastination, and overwhelming deadlines—but armed with the time management techniques you've learned, you have the power to overcome them. Remember the relatable quotes, inspiring success stories, and practical steps that have guided you in each chapter. They serve as reminders of the possibilities that lie ahead.

The path to academic success is not a solitary one. Seek support from your peers, mentors, and study groups. Embrace the joy of learning, celebrate your achievements, and find inspiration in the progress you make every day. Remember, even small steps forward are significant milestones on your journey.

Time management is not a one-size-fits-all approach. Explore different strategies, experiment with various techniques, and find what works best for you. Adapt and adjust as needed, recognizing that your time management needs may evolve as you grow and take on new challenges.

Embrace time management as more than just a tool for academic success. It is a lifelong skill that extends beyond the classroom. Apply the principles you've learned to your personal life, professional endeavours, and personal growth. Make time for self-care, prioritize your well-being, and find the harmony that allows you to thrive in all areas of your life.

As we conclude this book, remember that you are the author of your own time management story. Embrace the power of intentional choices, stay committed to your goals, and approach each day with enthusiasm and determination. Embrace the transformative potential of effective time management, and watch as it propels you toward greater heights of success.

May your college journey be filled with achievement, growth, and remarkable experiences. Use the knowledge and skills you have gained here to make the most of your time, create meaningful connections, and leave a lasting impact on your academic and personal life.

Thank you for joining me on this time management adventure. Remember, time is your most valuable asset—so use it wisely, cherish it, and let it become the foundation of your remarkable journey ahead. Go forth and conquer the world with the power of effective time management!"

Made in the USA
Columbia, SC
10 October 2024

43949476R00089